The Multidimensional Soul

*A Spiritual Awakening:
Path to Your Soul's Purpose*

by
Phillip Kayrouz and Leah Yiannis

© 2025 by Phillip Kayrouz and Leah Yiannis

All rights reserved. No part of this book may be reproduced in any manner whatsoever, including internet usage, without written permission from the authors, except in the case of brief quotations up to 250 words embodied in articles and reviews, with proper credit given to authors of The Multidimensional Soul book.

DISCLAIMER

The information given in this book should not be treated as a substitute for trained medical or psychological advice. The authors of this book do not dispense medical advice or prescribe the use of any technique as a form of treatment for physical or medical problems without the advice of a physician, either directly or indirectly. The intent of the author is only to offer information of a general nature to help you in your quest for emotional and spiritual well-being. Neither the authors nor the publisher can be held responsible for any loss, claim or damage arising out of the use, or misuse, of the suggestions made, the failure to take medical advice or for any material on third-party websites. Any use of information in this book is at the reader's discretion and risk.

DEDICATIONS

To my North Star, my beloved daughter and son, Jamal and Peter—this book is dedicated to you both, for you are the light that has guided me through every shadowed path. Your presence in my life has been a gift beyond words, a beacon that illuminated my way and helped me find my true self. Without you, I would have wandered lost, but with you, I have been blessed with purpose and clarity.

A special and heartfelt thanks to your mother, Marianne, whose strength, grace, and love gave you life and made this journey possible. It is because of her courage and the space she held for me to breathe and grow that I have been able to walk this path.

Eternally grateful, with all my heart.

Phillip

To my beloved Aunt Maria,
Your love and support shaped my life in ways I can never fully express. Your unexpected passing during my late teens marked a profound turning point, sparking a journey of spiritual awakening that continues to guide me. In life, you were a source of unwavering strength and care; in spirit, you have been a miraculous and inspiring presence, reminding me that we are eternal beings.
Thank you for showing me that love transcends time, space, and this earthly realm, and for continuing to light my path with your boundless love and infinite grace.

Leah

CONTENTS

Chapter 1: The Soul's Awakening — 11
What Is the Soul? — 11
Why Do Souls Exist? — 14
The Soul Beyond the Physical — 15
The Soul's Awakening — 17
Exercises — 19

Chapter 2: The Human Journey: Emotions as Energetic Transmutations — 23
Dark Night of the Soul — 23
Emotions as Gateways — 25
The Alchemy of Emotional Transformation — 27
Our Energy Centers and Transformation — 28
Engaging with the Higher Self — 31
Exercises — 33

Chapter 3: Soul: Trauma and Consciousness — 37
Trauma as a Catalyst for Transformation — 38
Energetic Fragmentation — 39
Trauma Healing as a Path to Ascension — 41
The Healing Journey: A Return to Wholeness — 43
Awakening Through Trauma — 45
Exercises — 47

Chapter 4: The Cosmic Soul — 50
Understanding the Cosmic Soul — 51
Spiritual Evolution & the Cosmic Soul — 52
Cosmic Soul & the Light Body — 53
Embracing the Spiral Path — 54
The Power of a Community of Healing — 54
Anchoring the Cosmic Soul in Daily Life — 54
Exercises — 56

CONTENTS

**Chapter 5: The Multidimensional Soul:
Beyond Space and Time** — 59

    Understanding the Essence of Who You Are — 59
    Soul Incarnation into Physical Form — 60
    Living Beyond the Physical — 60
    Signs of the Multidimensional Soul in Daily Life — 61
    Remembering Who We Are — 62
    The Quantum Nature of Reality — 63
    The Illusion of Separation and Time — 64
    The Ripple Effect: How Choices Shape Reality — 66
    Merging Timelines: Integrating the Self — 67
    Pathways to Higher Realms — 67
    Multidimensional Chakras & Emotional Healing — 68
    Fragments of Light and the Whole — 70
    The Holographic Principle: As Above, So Below — 71
    Holographic Healing and Integration — 72
    The Role of the Akashic Records — 73
    Ascension: From Duality to Unity — 75
    The Crystalline Grid — 76
    Conclusion - A Multidimensional Playground — 77
    A Living, Evolving Consciousness — 78
    The Magnetic Field and Earth's Lightbody — 79
    Humanity's Collective Role in Earth's Ascension — 80

**Chapter 6: Resources to Develop the
Multidimensional Soul** — 82

FORWARD

Dedicated to all the brave souls that put up their hands and agreed to come back to earth to continue the healing.

My personal journey began when the universe chose to exist and explore its own awareness. At that moment, the universe didn't fully understand itself until it created a spark of light to reveal contrast.

The Earth emerged as a living entity, and the universe recognised the need for special energies to support the fabric of existence. In turn, I've grown to realise that my soul engages in a cosmic dance; that I am woven into a wave-like existence that extends the depths and breadths of several realities.

Birthing into this human life, I later realised, was a commitment to lowering the vibrational frequency of my consciousness to attune to that of the earth's duality. At a particular point in my life leading up to this realisation, I agreed to awaken to my higher multidimensional self. Meanwhile... maintaining a 'normal' human life.

As I've learnt, and continue to learn about ancient spiritual communities, and their teachings of our connections with land, sky, and ancestors, I've begun to understand how each of us can breathe consciousness that is woven into the Earth itself.

Consciousness is an integral part of the Earth and provides a deep spiritual connection with the people and the land and seas. This connection is profound I've come to see. As communities intertwine with the environment, they are part of, and share a history with, a holistic view of existence emerges where nature and identity are inseparable.

This reflects a worldview I am now committed to; one that honours the relationships between people, their heritage, and the natural world. As such, I have a greater sense of responsibility and belonging in my life.

Working with Aboriginal communities over the past two years has deepened my understanding of this sacred connection. Their Elders teach that consciousness is woven into the very fabric of the Earth, creating an inseparable bond between land, sky, and ancestors. Through their stories of Dreamtime, they reveal how we transform not by changing our circumstances, but by aligning ourselves with life's natural rhythms.

Ancient wisdom tells us that the first Aboriginal peoples came as beings of light from the Pleiades, tasked with establishing Earth's energetic systems—particularly the heart, throat, and solar plexus chakras. As a dream walker and storyteller, I carry these teachings forward, recognising that every story shared becomes part of our collective awakening.

In sharing this work, I honour both my personal journey and the timeless wisdom of those who came before, understanding that we are all part of an unfolding cosmic narrative that connects us to the very essence of creation itself.

I remember the moment my soul came to life, and today I carry that spark as part of this human. As a dream walker, I traverse dimensions and realities, embracing the energy that flows through every layer of existence. This journey is not just personal; it is a communal one, deeply rooted in the teachings of my ancestors and of ancestors shared with me by others in story, ritual, dance, and art, as well as ontologies and epistemologies.

I understand that my cosmic blueprint allows me to embrace my spiritual heritage fully. The teachings remind me that I am a steward of this knowledge, carrying a legacy that spans generations. This stewardship is not a passive inheritance; it requires active engagement with cultural narratives and the integration of the wisdom of other inter-dimensional beings into my life.

The concept of individuation—a process of personal development involving the integration of various aspects of the self—parallels my journey. By exploring my unique blueprint and the stories that shape me, I embark on a path toward wholeness. This journey empowers me to confront my inner shadows, embrace my strengths, and navigate the complexities of existence with greater clarity.

I must highlight the importance of personal responsibility in shaping my destiny. When I embrace my role within this interconnected web, I recognise that my choices influence not only my own life but also the lives of others. This awareness has caused me to act with intention and compassion, fostering a sense of community that transcends my individual experiences.

In the cosmic dance of the soul, I find solace in knowing I am never alone. I am supported by the energies of my ancestors, the wisdom of the Elders, and the stories of those who came before me. By honouring these teachings and integrating them into my life, I step into my role as a custodian of my own soul and the collective spirit, dancing together in the sacred rhythms of life. Each movement I make enriches the grand tapestry of existence, reminding me of my profound connection to all that is. Through this exploration of the Cosmic Soul, I unlock the potential for personal and collective transformation, guiding me toward a more harmonious existence.

I believe this is the template of humanity narrated through Ancient history. Many souls form, with different functions, and those souls created for human lived lives are provided with a universal caretaker to watch over, nurture, love and support them.

As I align with my unique cosmic energies, I come to appreciate the beauty of my individual journey while recognising its place within the larger narrative of existence. This interconnectedness creates a sacred interplay where every action and intention reverberate through the web of life. Each step I take in this cosmic dance resonates beyond myself, contributing to the vibrancy of the world around me.

Phillip

CHAPTER 1
The Soul's Awakening

What Is the Soul?

The soul is the very essence of who we are— not an abstract concept or philosophical idea. It can be understood as the core of our consciousness and identity. Imagine the soul as a thread that connects you to everything: the Earth, the universe, and even something greater, such as the Divine (God). This thread symbolises interconnectedness, serving as a reminder that we are never truly alone but part of a much larger, interconnected picture.

This chapter introduces the fundamental concept of the soul as the core essence of consciousness that connects you to everything—the Earth, universe, and the Divine. How ancient cultures and modern thinkers have understood the soul as an immortal, evolving force that transcends physical existence, are explored. The ways in which the soul expresses itself through energy centres (chakras) and the awakening process as a journey of remembering our

Divine interconnectedness, are described. Through this awakening, we learn to align with universal principles and access higher states of consciousness, understanding that the soul's purpose is not to escape life but to grow through experiencing both light and shadow aspects of existence.

Ancient Soul Concepts

The journey to understanding your soul begins with one simple yet profound realisation, this book has endeavoured to convey: You are not only your body.

Your body is the physical manifestation of your being, but your soul is the eternal driver behind the wheel, a cosmic force experiencing life through the lens of physicality. The soul is often described as a spark of divine essence, an indestructible fragment of Source energy that retains consciousness across lifetimes and dimensions. But this is not just poetic sentiment. Many who have experienced deep meditation, astral travel, or near-death experiences, report encounters with their "higher self", a version of themselves that transcends time, space, and physical limitations.

In this expanded understanding, the soul is not static. It flows, shifts, and expands. Think of it like a beam of light that, when refracted through the prism of physical existence, splinters into countless colours.

Across ancient cultures, the soul was never perceived as something separate from the cosmos. Ancient thinkers and spiritual teachers have long explored the nature of the soul, often conceptualising it as a fragment of something eternal. For example, Plato proposed that the soul exists beyond the physical world, suggesting it is immortal and continues on beyond death. In modern thought, scientists like David Bohm view consciousness—what some scholars and spiritual traditions refer to as the soul—as part of a universal intelligence that shapes and organises reality.

In Egyptian tradition, the Ka (life force) and Ba (spirit) were believed to journey between worlds after death. Hindu texts describe the Atman, the unchanging core self, as part of Brahman, the universal consciousness. Indigenous cultures often saw the soul as part of the natural world, deeply connected to the cycles of the Earth, stars, and unseen realms. Shamans would enter trance states to communicate with soul fragments or spirits residing in alternate dimensions, further proving that the boundaries between the physical and the metaphysical were always permeable.

In Hermetic philosophy, the soul is understood as an immortal essence that serves as the bridge between the material body and the divine. The soul is believed to reflect the source of all creation, tasked with the journey of returning to its divine origin through growth, learning, and self-purification. It is this journey that allows the soul to ascend toward higher states of awareness by aligning itself with universal laws and divine truths. These laws include the Law of Vibration, and Law of Cause and Effect, which guide the soul's evolutionary path toward greater understanding and spiritual enlightenment.

This ancient and modern exploration of the soul reveals it to be far more than an abstract idea. The soul can be thought of as a living, evolving aspect of self, holding wisdom from countless experiences and capable of endless growth. It is both a personal journey and a universal one, representing the eternal thread that connects us to the divine, to each other, and to the entire cosmos.

From these philosophical and scientific perspectives, the soul emerges as something dynamic, alive, and continually evolving, drawing wisdom from countless experiences and existing within the fabric of universal consciousness.

A Sacred Connection

Many First Nations traditional cultures do not have a word for soul, rather, they speak of an inherent deep connection to the universe, past and present; others of us call this soul. These teachings remind us that our souls are not separate from the world but part of a living, breathing universe.

In today's busy world, this sacred connection is often forgotten. But the soul's light is never lost; it waits for us to remember. To awaken your soul is to reconnect with the rhythms of nature, the cosmos, and the divine energy that flows through everything.

Why Do Souls Exist?

The soul's purpose isn't to escape life but to grow and learn through it. Each experience teaches the soul something new, helping it to evolve. Awakening your soul isn't just about you, it also helps everyone around you as part of a greater, collective awakening.

When we awaken, we see that we're not separate from the universe. Instead, we're part of its grand symphony. This understanding changes how we see ourselves and inspires us to live with more kindness, awareness, and purpose.

The Soul as an Energetic Blueprint

Modern metaphysical teachings describe the soul as an energetic blueprint, intricately woven with the frequencies of multiple dimensions. While the body vibrates at the dense frequency of the third dimension (3D), the soul resonates across a much broader spectrum, reaching into higher planes of existence.

The energy field surrounding your body, often referred to as the aura, is an extension of this multidimensional blueprint. It carries the imprints of past lives, cosmic connections, and unfulfilled lessons. Your chakras, the energetic centers running along the spine, are points of intersection between the physical and the multidimensional, serving as gateways to the higher realms.

In essence, your body is the hardware, while the soul is the eternal software running across many devices at once.

The Soul Beyond the Physical

Your soul is not confined to your physical body or limited by the constraints of time and space; it exists as an eternal, boundless essence—an infinite energy that transcends earthly limitations. While the body is finite and subject to the physical world's constraints, your soul is limitless, eternal, and interconnected with the universal intelligence that governs all existence. Awakening your soul, therefore, is not merely about personal development or healing; it is about establishing a profound connection with the infinite intelligence of the universe and remembering your soul's divine purpose and origins.

The soul is far more than our physical experiences; it is the unbroken thread connecting us to the infinite, timeless dimension of existence. By allowing ourselves to listen—to the stillness, to the patterns of energy, and to the deep inner knowing—we can respond to the soul's invitation to awaken. This awakening is a journey toward higher states of consciousness, spiritual alignment, and ultimately, the realisation that we are more than our physical bodies: we are eternal beings connected to the vast, interconnected web of universal intelligence and divine purpose.

The soul expresses itself through energy centers known as chakras. These centers serve as gateways for life force energy, each governing different aspects of our physical, emotional, and spiritual well-being:

1. **Root Chakra** (Muladhara): Grounds us in physical existence
2. **Sacral Chakra** (Svadhisthana): Governs creativity and emotions
3. **Solar Plexus** Chakra (Manipura): Centers personal power
4. **Heart Chakra** (Anahata): Opens us to love and compassion
5. **Throat Chakra** (Vishuddha): Enables truthful expression
6. **Third Eye Chakra** (Ajna): Awakens intuition and insight
7. **Crown Chakra** (Sahasrara): Connects us to divine wisdom

Understanding these energy centers provides a framework for soul development and spiritual growth.

The Soul's Awakening

A soul awakening represents a profound process of rediscovery—a journey back to the essential truth of our divine interconnectedness. This awakening is not about acquiring new information but about remembering the inherent knowledge and connection that resides within each of us. It's a return to the understanding that the soul is not isolated but intricately woven into the fabric of all existence, connected to the Earth, the universe, and the Divine.

A soul's awakening involves transcending the illusion of separation—the feeling that we are solely individual physical beings—and recognising the deeper, universal oneness. The journey is a call to explore the dualities of life—the highs and lows, joy and sorrow, light and shadow—through which the soul gains wisdom and integration. As individuals confront these experiences, they begin to dismantle the fear-based or limiting beliefs that keep them from fully accessing their higher consciousness.

The Essenes, an ancient spiritual and mystical group, also understood this concept. They taught that the soul's journey is an evolutionary path toward spiritual illumination and healing through alignment with divine truth and universal law. In their teachings, the soul's awakening is a process of purification, self-awareness, and unity with divine energies. It requires embracing both the light and the shadow aspects of our being as opportunities for transformation and integration. Through this process, the soul comes into greater alignment with higher spiritual truths and the natural order of the cosmos.

A soul awakening, therefore, is an invitation to let go of

fear, surrender to divine guidance, and step into a state of remembrance—a reactivation of the soul's original blueprint and connection to all that is. It is the realisation that we are more than our physical bodies or individual identities; we are fragments of the divine, here to experience, learn, and return to the understanding of oneness. This awakening allows individuals to embody their higher selves, access deeper levels of intuition, and align their lives with a greater spiritual purpose.

Ultimately, through soul awakening, one learns to live in harmony with the universal principles of balance, love, and unity. It is a sacred journey of remembering that we are all interconnected, that every experience holds meaning, and that the soul's purpose is to heal, evolve, and return to the divine source through conscious self-discovery and spiritual growth.

Teachings like The Law of One say the soul is part of a single, unified energy that's always learning and growing and about finding balance in life's opposites. It's in facing these contrasts that the soul becomes stronger and wiser.

As the poet Khalil Gibran wrote,

> "Your soul is oftentimes a battlefield, where your reason and your judgment wage war against your passion and your appetite."

To awaken your soul, you must face these challenges and peel away what's false, finding the true, Divine spark within.

What's Next?

In the next chapter, we'll explore how to remember who we truly are and take the first steps toward awakening the soul.

This journey is one of transformation. It heals us personally and helps us understand our unique role in the beautiful, endless dance of existence.

The soul's invitation is clear: *wake up, remember your true nature, and reconnect with the sacred energy of life.*

By doing this, you'll discover your purpose, your truth, and your place in the vast and wondrous universe.

Meanwhile, reflecting on the concept of the soul can be a deeply personal and transformative experience. Here are several reflective activities to explore the idea of the soul, tailored for different levels of introspection and engagement.

Journaling Prompts

- **Daily Reflection:** Write about moments that felt deeply meaningful or "bigger than yourself." What might they reveal about your soul?

- **Soul's Essence:** Reflect on the question, "Who am I beyond my roles, achievements, and possessions?"

- **Life's Purpose:** Consider, "What do I feel called to do in this life? What lights me up and makes me feel alive?"

- **Inner Wisdom:** Journal about times when you felt guided by an inner voice or intuition. Could this be the voice of your soul?

Mindfulness and Meditation

- **Soul Meditation:** Sit quietly, focusing on your breath. Imagine a light or warmth at your core, representing your soul. Observe how this energy feels and where it seems to lead your thoughts or emotions.

- **Nature Connection:** Spend time in nature, focusing on your connection to the Earth. Reflect on how the beauty and rhythms of the natural world might mirror the flow of your soul.
- **Loving-Kindness Meditation:** Extend feelings of love and compassion to yourself and others, imagining your soul radiating this energy outward.

Creative Expression

- **Art or Poetry:** Create a piece of art or write a poem that expresses your understanding or experience of the soul. Don't focus on making it perfect, let it flow from your intuition.
- **Music:** Listen to music that stirs your emotions and reflect on why it resonates with you. Does it feel like it speaks to your soul?
- **Storytelling:** Write or imagine a story about your soul's journey through life. What challenges has it faced? What wisdom has it gained?

Spiritual or Philosophical Exploration

- **Sacred Texts**: Read excerpts from spiritual or philosophical texts (e.g., Rumi, the Bhagavad Gita, the Bible, or works by modern thinkers). Reflect on how they describe the soul and its purpose.
- **Teachings of Mystics**: Study ideas from mystics like Alan Watts, Eckhart Tolle, or Indigenous wisdom traditions. How do their perspectives resonate with your own?

- **Soul Inquiry:** Explore questions like "Is the soul eternal?" or "How does the soul influence my actions and choices?" and write your evolving thoughts.

Guided Activities

- **Inner Child Work:** Reflect on what your younger self would say about who you are now. How does this connect to your soul's essence?
- **Life Mapping:** Create a timeline of your life's most meaningful experiences. Identify patterns or lessons that seem to reflect the journey of your soul.
- **Gratitude Practice:** List things you're grateful for and consider how each might nurture your soul.

Connection with Others

- **Deep Conversations:** Discuss the concept of the soul with a trusted friend or group. How do their perspectives expand your understanding?
- **Acts of Service:** Engage in activities that help others or the environment. Reflect on how giving of yourself feels like an expression of your soul.

Rituals and Ceremonies

- **Lighting a Candle:** Light a candle in a quiet space and meditate on its flame as a symbol of your soul.
- **Earth Ritual:** Plant a tree, tend to a garden, or perform a grounding ritual outdoors. Reflect on your soul's connection to the Earth and its cycles.
- **Creative Altar:** Build an altar with objects that feel meaningful to you. Use it as a space to reflect on your soul's presence in your life.

Dream Work

- **Dream Journaling:** Record your dreams and look for symbols or patterns that might reflect your soul's desires or messages.
- **Lucid Dreaming Practice:** Try to become aware in your dreams and explore questions about your soul while dreaming.

Physical Activities

- **Mindful Movement:** Engage in yoga, tai chi, or walking meditation. Focus on how your body feels as a vessel for your soul.
- **Dance:** Allow your body to move freely to music, expressing whatever comes up without judgment. Reflect on how this feels like a connection to your deeper self.

Each of these activities provides an opportunity to pause, listen, and connect with what feels most authentic and meaningful in your life, a journey many would describe as the awakening of the soul.

CHAPTER 2:
The Human Journey: Emotions as Energetic Transmutations

The journey of awakening the soul is not about escaping life but about embracing it fully—learning, growing, and remembering all that we are. As we begin this journey, we recognise that to fully awaken and reconnect with our divine essence, we must confront the emotional and shadow aspects of our human experience. Emotions are not mere fleeting reactions; they are dynamic energies woven into the fabric of our human existence.

This chapter invites you to be curious about these emotional energies, and to develop an understanding of how they serve both as veils that obscure our true nature, and as gateways that lead us toward self-realisation and the integration of the soul. The purpose of this chapter is to encourage you to process and where needed, embrace emotions that can be a catalyst for your inner harmony, through spiritual awakening and the reclamation of your authentic self.

Dark Night of the Soul

The process of the Dark Night of the Soul is a transformative passage where suppressed emotions like fear, anger, and sadness come to the surface. These emotions are not obstacles but gateways; they invite us to explore the depths of our conditioning, release what no longer serves us, and integrate these emotional energies into wholeness. Through this journey, the soul learns to navigate human nature and find balance, creating the space to remember its purpose and reconnect with universal truths. This is not just a personal path but part of a greater, collective journey toward awakening and remembering our interconnectedness with the symphony of the universe.

The Dark Night of the Soul represents a symbolic death and rebirth. The shedding of old skins (ways of being) and a harmonising of dualities (positive and negative emotions). It is a profound initiation into deeper levels of consciousness, where illusions are stripped away, and the true essence of being as a human, is unveiled. This unveiling requires the psyche to be brought into the foreground (into your conscious awareness) of this lived human experience. It is in the moments of despair, when the weight of pain feels unbearable, that we are invited to pause, to truly be present with our emotions, rather than turning away from them.

In the grand tapestry of life, the Dark Night of the Soul emerges as a profound spiritual odyssey - a sacred passage where deep-seated emotions like anger, sadness, and fear surface, yearning to be acknowledged and transformed.

Characteristics of the Dark Night of the Soul can include:
- Deep questioning of life's meaning
- Confrontation with shadow aspects
- Release of old emotional patterns
- Emergence of higher awareness

This passage, though challenging, serves as a crucial catalyst for spiritual evolution and emotional mastery.

Emotions as Gateways

Emotions are windows into our energetic landscape. Acknowledging emotions such as grief, anger, or fear can reveal precisely where the energy body is blocked. If we bypass or suppress these feelings, we risk trapping these vibrations even deeper in our subtle fields.

Facing these emotions, with gentleness and curiosity, allows the energetic knots to loosen. Once released or transformed, the energetic flow becomes more harmonious, and the soul experiences a renewed sense of equilibrium. This emotional aspect is intimately connected with our subtle energy bodies, reminding us that psychic and emotional healing are deeply intertwined.

Consider this story about Anna, a high-powered executive engulfed by profound sadness after her sister's death. In the latter stages of her grief cycle, her grief became a catalyst for introspection. She was prompted to question her life's purpose. By surrendering to her sadness rather than resisting it, Anna embarked on a transformative journey. She modified her stressful work schedule, sought counselling, and pursued a childhood dream to learn and excel in tennis. Overall, Anna found herself aligning with her soul's purpose, and life began to provide her with a sense of fulfillment she had never known before.

The Energetic Essence of Emotions

Each emotion carries within it a unique vibrational signature, a reflection of the state of our inner cosmos. Sadness often links us to loss and a deep yearning for the divine, inviting us to release and surrender. This makes room for our new growth. For example, anger can be a beacon, illuminating areas of inner resistance or stagnation. The emotion can highlight where our boundaries have been crossed, offering profound lessons in self-expression and self-advocacy. Alternatively, fear often mirrors our disconnection from a sense of trust and safety in our personal spaces. Engaging with this emotion can urge us toward acts of courage and allowing ourselves to be vulnerable (with reasonable discernment).

As Alan Watts eloquently shares, embracing all aspects of our experience, including emotions we are uncomfortable with (when not in mortal danger), is essential for transcending the illusion of separation. By reconciling the opposites within ourselves, we move toward wholeness. Emotions, then, are not obstacles but integral challenges which are crucial parts of the human journey. They can guide us back to the unity from which we all originate.

By acknowledging the depth of our struggle, we release the grip of the ego, which seeks control and avoidance. In this gentle presence, we allow ourselves to be vulnerable and open, creating space for healing and transformation. Love, in its purest form, is not about escaping hardship but embracing it fully, knowing that through surrender, we transcend and acknowledging rather than ignoring the void, can relinquish egoic control and be liberating.

As you move through this time of deep healing and transformation, you may encounter paradoxes and strange synchronicities that push you toward a metaphorical death—a letting go of old beliefs and ways of being. This experience is necessary to help you awaken to the truth that you are a spirit having a human experience, and it is through this process that you find deeper self-awareness and healing.

The Alchemy of Emotional Transformation

Emotional alchemy involves consciously working with emotional energies to transmute lower frequencies into higher states of awareness. This process requires:

1. **Recognition:** Acknowledging emotions without judgment
2. **Presence:** Staying with the emotional energy as it moves through
3. **Transmutation:** Consciously shifting the energy toward higher frequencies
4. **Integration:** Incorporating the wisdom gained from the process

Anger: The Alchemical Fire

Anger is often misunderstood and misjudged, for at times, it holds immense transformative power. It tends to arise when our boundaries are breached, our desires are unmet, or we perceive injustices to ourselves or another. However, when we approach anger with curiosity and respect, it becomes an alchemical force for personal evolution, transmuting base emotions into higher understanding.

Anger often springs from the ego's desire for separation and control. Unchecked, it can obscure our inner light and perpetuate cycles of suffering, for ourselves and sometimes others too. Yet, within anger lies a powerful summons for healing. Carl Jung's concept of the "Shadow" represents the unconscious parts of ourselves that we suppress or deny. By acknowledging and befriending our shadow, we can dissolve the barriers between the conscious and unconscious mind, leading to wholeness.

In shamanic traditions, anger can highlight fragmented aspects of the soul, guiding us toward retrieval and integration of these lost pieces. Emotional mastery can orient us with universal truth. Anger, akin to fire, has the power to destroy yet also to purify.

Alan Watts emphasises that to achieve comprehensive understanding of ourselves, we must reconcile the dualities within us. Embracing both light and dark sides of ourselves in terms of the lessons they can bring us. Joy and sorrow can help us to transcend limitations of the ego and experience the deeper reality of life. The Phoenix Archetype embodies this transformation: Through the flames of destruction comes rebirth, mirroring our potential for renewal by letting go of that which no longer serves us and the broader community.

By facing our shadow, we transcend the paradox of the dualities which confine us from experiencing the true nature of reality. Emotional clearing techniques, such as addressing stored emotions in the subtle energy bodies and healing fractures in the soul caused by trauma, can facilitate this profound integration.

Ignoring emotional wounds can lead to psychological distortions like anxiety, depression, or destructive behaviors, as energetic imbalances manifest on the physical and conscious dimension. Therefore, engaging in shadow work becomes an essential step toward healing and integration.

Our Energy Centres & Transformation

By accepting life's paradoxes and recognising that opposing forces can coexist, we can move through the dark night of the soul and our feeling of suffering through living with purpose and connecting with the infinite. As part of this healing process, your energy centres will begin to awaken. These centres, known as chakras, have been understood for centuries by ancient traditions. Some teachings, like those in the Law of One, explain and align the chakras as key to understanding and balancing our spiritual and physical selves.

The teachings of The Law of One, a framework for energy centres (chakras) within us. Each energy centre corresponds to a different level of consciousness, a different aspect of spiritual development.

According to The Law of One, the human energy system consists of seven primary energy centres:

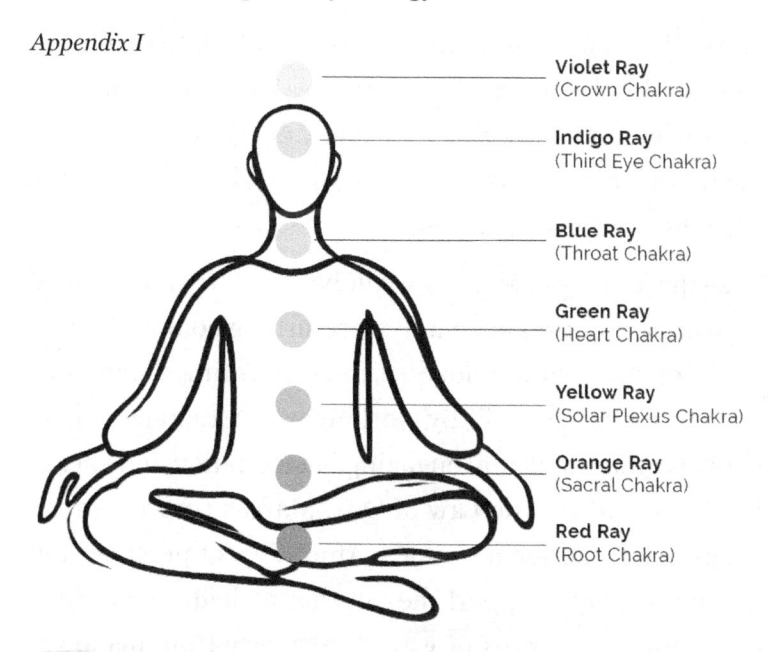

Appendix I

Violet Ray
(Crown Chakra)

Indigo Ray
(Third Eye Chakra)

Blue Ray
(Throat Chakra)

Green Ray
(Heart Chakra)

Yellow Ray
(Solar Plexus Chakra)

Orange Ray
(Sacral Chakra)

Red Ray
(Root Chakra)

1. **Red Ray** (Root Chakra): Governs survival, grounding, and the foundation of physical existence.

2. **Orange Ray** (Sacral Chakra): Relates to personal identity, emotions, and creativity.

3. **Yellow Ray** (Solar Plexus Chakra): Associated with personal power, will, and social roles.

4. **Green Ray** (Heart Chakra): Centres on love, compassion, and healing.

5. **Blue Ray** (Throat Chakra): Involves communication, truth, and expression.

6. **Indigo Ray** (Third Eye Chakra): Connection with intuition, insight, and higher wisdom.

7. **Violet Ray** (Crown Chakra): Reflects spiritual connection and unity consciousness.

Unresolved emotional experiences can block these energy centres, hindering spiritual growth. By confronting and healing emotional wounds, we allow energy to flow freely, facilitating personal transformation and aligning ourselves with the universal consciousness.

Take the journey of Marcus, a combat veteran who grappled with intense anger and fear upon returning home. His Dark Night of the Soul unfolded through haunting nightmares and emotional turmoil. By working with a therapist along with learning about and engaging in meditation and energy healing based on The Law of One, Marcus confronted his suppressed emotional wounds. After diligent practice, and finding the right support, he felt that he had cleansed his traumatic experiences of war, particularly from his lower three chakras (root, sacral, and solar). This courageous process led him back to an inner peace and a renewed sense of purpose he had not experienced since the birth of his children many years earlier.

The Path of Integration and Wholeness

Healing can unfold through the acknowledgment and integration of our emotional dualities, rather than through their suppression or by being consumed by them. This sacred work involves engaging with various practices that address the multidimensional aspects of our being.

Emotional healing practices, such as auric clearing and timeline integration, can remove energetic attachments and heal traumas from past lives (timelines) affecting our present. Practical tools, such as meditation, visualisation, and journaling allow us to anchor awareness in higher vibrations, connecting us with multidimensional aspects of ourselves. Journaling especially enables exploration of emotional patterns and recording of breakthroughs. While energy cleansing through smudging, sound healing, or working with crystals, can maintain the purity of our energetic field.

Consider Sophia's journey of self-integration using the multidimensional soul techniques. Her suppressed anger had manifested as chronic self-doubt and indecision in her personal life. Through auric clearing and timeline healing, she reconnected with her higher chakras, and slowly integrated fragmented aspects of her soul. This profound process restored her confidence and clarity of purpose in daily functioning and inter-personal relationships.

Engaging with the Higher Self

Connecting with your Higher Self brings clarity and guidance beyond the limitations of the ego. The Higher Self is our true nature, beyond the confines of identity, a pure expression of the universe experiencing itself.

As you heal and integrate your emotions, you naturally expand into a sense of oneness with all life. The Law of One teaches that all is one, separation is an illusion as all beings are interconnected. When aligned with unity consciousness, we naturally act with compassion and love, for ourselves and others.

We are as human beings, the universe experiencing itself. Embracing this claim can dissolve purposeless suffering, allowing us to live from a place of profound connection to ourselves, our environment, and to others.

The journey through your emotional wounds is not a straight line but a spiral, revisiting themes at deeper levels across iterations. Each encounter offers new insights and opportunities for transformation. Trust the process, having faith in the inner wisdom of the universe and the unfolding of your path.

By reconciling opposites and embracing all aspects of yourself, you move toward integration and transcendence. By dissolving illusions and experiencing raw reality, we find liberation. The multidimensional teachings of the ancients and The Law of One provide tools for this journey. Guiding us toward the wholeness that is our birthright.

Embracing and transforming emotions is a lifelong journey, a sacred dance between the human and the divine within each of us. By engaging with these practices and integrating insights of our multidimensional soul we honour every aspect of our being. Each step brings you closer to the realisation of unity and divine purpose; where the self merges with the cosmos in a harmonious symphony of existence. We can then manifest this harmony in our day to day 'mundane' lives, bringing wholeness and meaning, despite the obstacles.

What's Next?

In the next chapter, you'll explore how trauma can shape consciousness and influence the soul's journey. While emotions serve as powerful catalysts for transformation, understanding how trauma affects our energetic blueprint helps us navigate deeper waters of healing. This exploration will reveal how wounds can become profound teachers, leading us toward greater wholeness and integration.

By understanding and healing trauma, space is created for the authentic self to emerge. Through this process, the deepest wounds can serve as gateways to awakening and accessing the wisdom that resides within the soul's vast landscape.

Reflecting on emotions as energetic forces can be a deeply personal and transformative experience. Here are several reflective activities to explore your emotional landscape, tailored for different levels of understanding and engagement

Journaling Journey

Reflect on a recent time when an overwhelming emotion surfaced in your life. Describe the situation in detail, allowing yourself to fully experience the memory and emotion with as little positive or negative judgment as possible.

- What insights emerge for you about this experience?

- Consider how this emotion has or has not, reshaped your perspective about your life's purpose.
- Reflect on this introspection exercise, has it or has it not aided you in uncovering veils of understanding about yourself and your path? How so?

Reflective Meditation

Contemplate the question: What could my anger be revealing about my unmet needs, core values, and objective reality?" Find a quiet space where you can meditate by sitting quietly and turning your focus inwards and allow the anger to speak to you, what does it want you to know? What does it need from you? Become the neutral observer and be curious without judgment. Simply listen or write freely for 15 minutes. Allow your thoughts and feelings to flow without overly censoring them, and from a place of compassion.

Shadow Work Journaling

Identify emotional stressors by listing situations that provoke strong reactions within you (positive and negative). Explore the underlying beliefs you have about each situation. Practice self-compassion, offering understanding and kindness to wounded parts of yourself. Visualise cultivating a relationship with these aspects of yourself; acknowledging their role in your survival, growth, and shadow integration.

Higher Self Meditation

Create a sacred space by lighting candles or incense, signifying the beginning of a special time. Relax deeply through breathwork, releasing tension with each exhale. Visualise a serene environment where you feel at peace, a garden, a beach, or a starlit sky. Invite your Higher Self to join you, envisioning a luminous, loving presence approaching. Engage in a dialogue, asking questions and seeking guidance on emotional challenges. Stay open to receiving insights through thoughts, feelings, or images. Express gratitude for the wisdom shared, and gently bring your awareness back, feeling centered and enlightened. Consider journaling your experience.

Oneness Meditation

Find a natural setting (if possible), a forest, a park, or even a quiet room with elements of nature such as a vase with garden fronds or flowers. Begin by connecting with your breath, inhaling deeply and imagining that you are breathing in the energy of the Earth. With each exhale, feel your energy merging with all that is around you. Silently repeat the affirmation, "I am one with the universe; the universe is one with me." Allow this sense of unity to permeate your being, sustaining the feeling for as long as you are comfortable. Consider journalling about your experience.

Timeline Healing Meditation

Set an intention to heal across all timelines, declaring your desire with conviction in your journal. Next, enter a meditative state using deep breathing to relax your body and mind. Visualise your timeline as a path representing your soul's journey. Notice obstacles you've navigated along this path which have left you feeling depleted or meaningless. Apply healing energy by sending light and compassion to these aspects of you, your past self. Welcome returning soul fragments with love and compassion, integrating them into your multidimensional being. Conclude by expressing gratitude to your past self and any spiritual guides who assisted along your timeline.

CHAPTER 3:
SOUL: Trauma and Consciousness

Trauma can be characterised as a wound. Yet it is also an energetic experience that reshapes our sense of self. When we speak of the soul, we address the continuous thread of our being that spans physical, emotional, mental, and spiritual dimensions. Trauma can disrupt this continuum, creating discord in how energy flows both within our personal field, and in the fields of those we interact with.

Though challenging, trauma can also serve as a gateway to deeper spiritual understanding. Rather than only being a psychological interruption, it can be viewed as an initiatory process that draws our attention to energetic imprints. By contemplating trauma through the lens of energy, we begin to see how this disruption can be harnessed for transformation. In acknowledging the depth of trauma's influence on our lives, we also open ourselves to the possibility of healing at a multidimensional level. This facilitates our personal growth and can contribute to our ascension to the Divine.

This chapter explores trauma as an energetic experience that can disrupt the soul's natural flow. However, it can also serve as a gateway to deeper spiritual understanding and transformation. Through examining trauma from an energetic perspective, we learn how it affects a person's subtle bodies and chakras, creating blockages that can manifest in various aspects of life. Yet, also offering opportunities for profound healing and growth.

The chapter explains how trauma healing becomes a path to ascension, recovering lrecover lost soul fragments and raising vibrational frequency, contributing to both personal and collective evolution. Through practices like soul retrieval, energy healing, and conscious integration, trauma's dense energetic imprints can be transformed into catalysts for awakening, wholeness, and connection with the Divine.

Trauma & Its Interaction with the Soul

Trauma is more than an emotional crisis; it is an energetic rupture. When we endure a highly distressing event, or series of events, our energy body may undergo shock, causing fragmentation of the soul's natural flow. Rather than existing in the harmonious frequency of our authentic state, we may become stuck in denser vibrations associated with fear, pain, or unprocessed emotion.

Trauma as a Catalyst for Transformation

Despite trauma's challenging nature, it possesses the potential to awaken us to deeper truths. Many spiritual teachings propose that every painful event contains a seed for growth and reintegration. In energetic terms, when the soul's flow is disrupted, it calls us to address that disruption consciously. The invitation is to process and transmute the denser, heavier vibrations into more balanced, higher-frequency states.

Trauma thus presents a mirror: a chance to confront our shadow or the aspects of ourselves that lie in darkness. If we stay in denial, we risk deepening the energetic fracture. However, by acknowledging and working through these wounded aspects, we begin to alchemise fear into understanding, anger into empowerment, and victimhood into self-sovereignty.

Energetic Fragmentation

This fragmentation registers at subtle levels of the aura and in our energy centres (chakras). The energy centres can become blocked or sluggish when confronted with unresolved trauma. Over time, these blockages embed themselves into our subtle fields, influencing our physical health, emotional wellness, and spiritual clarity.

From an energetic viewpoint, ascension refers to the elevation of consciousness toward higher vibrational states. As an individual clears trauma, their personal frequency increases. This internal shift echoes outward, interacting with the collective consciousness. Energetic healing is never an isolated act; when one person heals, the ripple effect can subtly uplift those around them.

Trauma disrupts the cohesion between the physical body, the spiritual essence, and our cosmic body. The energetic template that connects us with universal energies. When traumatic events occur, the shock waves can reverberate across these layers, storing dense energetic imprints that linger long after the initial event.

These imprints often remain beneath conscious awareness, manifesting as anxiety, recurrent nightmares, or even chronic health issues. Because the human energy system is deeply interconnected, blockages in one area can cause resonant disturbances in another. For instance, if the root energy centre (associated with survival and grounding) absorbs traumatic energy, we may experience persistent fears around safety or basic security. Over time, if unaddressed, these energetic blockages can ripple upward through the body, affecting everything from emotional stability to mental clarity.

While the energy centres as a seven-chakra model is most commonly known. There are additional energy centers, such as the Earth Star Chakra (below the feet) and higher transpersonal chakras like the Soul Star Chakra or Stellar Gateway (above the crown). Trauma can affect any or all of these centers, restricting the flow of higher consciousness into our everyday awareness.

- **Earth Star Chakra:** This centre grounds us to the planet's energies. Trauma can block this chakra, leaving us feeling disconnected from our physical environment.
- **Root Chakra:** Stores fundamental fears and issues of survival. Energetic imprints here can manifest as persistent worry, hypervigilance, or chronic insecurity.
- **Heart Chakra:** Governs connection and compassion. Trauma lodged here might lead to difficulty expressing love, trust, or openness.
- **Soul Star Chakra:** Represents our bridge to higher wisdom and collective consciousness. When disrupted by trauma, it can feel as though we've lost the sense of a bigger cosmic purpose or guidance.

By engaging in practices that balance and cleanse these centers, we facilitate the free flow of energy throughout the multidimensional system, ultimately reintegrating the fragments of our soul. This process involves clearing dense layers of stuck emotion and welcoming in higher-frequency vibrations that support healing and expansion.

Practices such as meditation, Qi gong, or community-based energy healing amplify these shifts. By fostering coherence in one's energy field and deliberately sharing that coherence in group meditations or healing circles, each person contributes to an ever-expanding network of higher vibrational frequencies. Over time, this collective ascension supports more harmonious social structures and a deeper mutual understanding across communities and cultures.

Trauma Healing as a Path to Ascension

Ascension is a transformative process of raising one's vibrational frequency, allowing the soul to expand into higher realms of consciousness. This journey involves the clearing of deep-seated emotions, including experiences of trauma. As such, ascension can aid the dissolution of our limiting beliefs, and enable regulation of the ego (i.e., recognising its value while ensuring it does not dominate our experiences of self).

Ascension can manifest as periods of intense emotional release, heightened awareness, or profound spiritual insights. A person may experience synchronicities, a deep sense of interconnectedness, or a shift in perception of reality. For example, you may notice negative recurring patterns in life begin to dissolve, and relationships shift toward greater harmony. Or you may have moments of clarity that reveal your soul's purpose. A clear sign of ascension is the ability to remain present and grounded while navigating challenges with greater compassion and balanced perspective. This reflects your soul's alignment with higher frequencies.

This balance of perspective may be described by some as 'detachment'. In this context, it is often misunderstood as a lack of care or interest. Rather, the balance of how you perceive and interpret experiences is not about becoming indifferent or disengaged. Rather, it is the intentional conscious practice of observing experiences without being overwhelmed by them.

This balance allows us to respond with clarity and compassion, rather than reacting impulsively or avoiding the reality before us. Unlike apathy, which signals disinterest, a balanced perspective reflects a deep connection to the present moment, and the ability to witness events from a place of inner peace. Be the eye in the storm. To do this requires trusting the flow of life and your place in it. Accepting outcomes while recognising that challenges, failures, and adversity are part of the journey.

This balanced perspective allows for personal growth, resilience, and the ability to navigate life's complexities with grace. It acknowledges that while some external events may be beyond our control, and some internal responses overly influence our experience, we have the potential to discover ways to manage our journey through the obstacles.

Embracing this reality fosters self-compassion, allowing us to engage with our healing journey without unrealistic expectations. The journey toward healing is not linear, and allowing space for difficult emotions and thoughts is part of the process. Recognising that setbacks or moments of despair are natural, but do not need to be "the end of the road", creates room for eventual growth, resilience, and light body ascension.

For example, anger often highlights areas of disempowerment or soul fragmentation in our life. By embracing rather than suppressing this emotion, we reclaim lost aspects of ourselves, fostering greater wholeness. This recalls for us the Dark Night of the Soul discussed in the previous chapter. The Healing Journey: A Return to Wholeness

In shamanic traditions and other esoteric frameworks, trauma is often said to cause "soul loss," wherein pieces of one's essence detach and remain frozen in time. Beyond metaphor, this concept points to very real energetic disruptions within the aura and energy centres.

Techniques like soul retrieval are designed to bring back these scattered parts, restoring our inherent wholeness. During soul retrieval, practitioners enter altered states of consciousness to locate these fragments and reintegrate them into the individual's energy field.

Though less emphasis is placed here on specific recovery protocols, the key is to recognise that trauma clearing is about releasing old energy which no longer serves us, and welcoming home lost or exiled aspects of the self. Healing becomes a sacred return, a guided reconnection to our soul's eternal state.

The Healing Journey: A Return to Wholeness

Ultimately, healing trauma from an energetic perspective is

a reclamation of our innate wholeness. While trauma may momentarily obscure our soul's light, it never extinguishes it. This journey back to wholeness is both personal and collective. As individuals elevate their frequency by clearing trauma, the cumulative effect resonates through families, communities, and even the planet at large. The microcosm of personal healing interacts with the macrocosm of universal consciousness, reflecting the non-dual nature of energy: what happens within us simultaneously affects the external world.

An unresolved emotion such as fear, shame, or guilt can manifest in actions that perpetuate limiting patterns. When we speak harshly or act from a place of wounding, we emit a frequency that reverberates in our surroundings. Conversely, conscious behaviours rooted in compassion and understanding broadcast a higher vibrational state.

In the context of trauma, persistent negative behaviours often trace back to energetic disruptions formed at the time of the traumatic event. By addressing the imbalances in the subtle bodies, we can move beyond mere behaviour modification and reach the root causes, transforming the energetic residue that fuels unhealthy patterns.

Trauma as a Teacher: Learning from Darkness

Trauma introduces us to our own darkness, the aspects of ourselves that may remain hidden until forced into the light by adversity. While painful, these darker experiences can illuminate our capacity for resilience and deeper insight. From an energy perspective, darkness is not merely a void or "bad energy"; it is an invitation to alchemise that frequency into something more aligned with our core truth.

In many spiritual traditions, the Phoenix rising from ashes symbolises this process: transformation follows disintegration. Here, trauma represents the ashes, the residue of an old state of being, and the transformation arises from the intentional clearing and re-harmonising of that energy. The journey leads to rebirth: the self emerges freer and more aware, possibly carrying new spiritual gifts uncovered by the healing process.

Awakening Through Trauma

The experience of trauma can serve as a wake-up call to dimensions of consciousness previously overlooked. Dreams may become more vivid, psychic abilities may sharpen, or synchronistic events might increase. These phenomena highlight the soul's innate capacity to guide our healing. The presence of ancestral or cosmic support is also frequently reported: individuals sense benevolent forces aiding them in reclaiming lost parts of themselves.

This awakening underscores the interconnectedness of all beings and the reality that healing radiates outward. Every shift in personal consciousness cascades into shifts in the collective, reinforcing the notion that trauma, while difficult, is also a pathway to collective evolution.

Trauma, viewed through the framework of energy, reveals a tapestry of disruption and potential. It fractures our multidimensional bodies and scatters aspects of our soul, lodging dense vibrations into chakras and subtle fields. Yet the very process of fragmentation highlights the soul's innate capacity for healing and expansion. Recognising trauma's energetic dimensions opens new pathways for understanding how transformation takes place. Not just psychologically, but also at subtle and invisible layers of our being.

Embracing the challenge of trauma invites us to reclaim lost fragments, attune to higher frequencies, and harmonise our energy centers for deeper spiritual integration. As we heal individually, our elevated vibrations ripple throughout the collective, playing a role in humanity's collective ascension. This synergy between personal and collective healing reflects an unbreakable interconnectedness. In essence, clearing dense energy from trauma allows the light of the soul to shine more brightly, reminding us of our eternal nature.

Practical applications like soul retrieval, energy centre meditations, and emotional processing cannot be separated from the broader psycho-spiritual process. Their significance lies in demonstrating that trauma recovery is not merely about mending what was broken, but also about reclaiming the fullness of who we are. By viewing trauma through the lens of energy, we discover that every challenging event holds within it an invitation for deeper self-discovery and reintegration.

The soul's journey through trauma is ultimately a path of becoming more fully alive and connected... to our self. Also, to others and the vast universal field of consciousness beyond our physical being. , to each other, and to the vast universal field of consciousness. Through healing our energetic bodies, we enter a state of greater alignment with our own divine essence, transcending the limitations once imposed by pain and fragmentation. In doing so, we transform our personal stories. We also contribute to the ever-evolving fabric of humanity's collective ascension.

What's Next?

In the next chapter, you'll explore the vast cosmic dimension of our soul—our connection to the stars, higher realms, and the infinite web of creation. Through understanding our cosmic nature, we discover that our earthly experiences, including trauma and healing, are part of a greater journey that spans dimensions and star systems.

As we open to this expanded awareness, we begin to recognise ourselves as beings of light temporarily experiencing human form, with access to profound wisdom and universal consciousness that can guide our evolution and transformation.

Consideration of trauma through an energetic lens can be a deeply personal and transformative experience. The following activities provide different pathways to explore your own or to support another's healing journey. Each activity provides a unique way to reconnect with and reintegrate aspects of soul.

These practices are designed to support at whatever stage of healing resonates for you or the person you are providing a healing space to.

Guided Visualisation for Soul Retrieval

- **Preparation:** Find a quiet, comfortable space and set a clear intention, such as "I am open to retrieving and integrating the fragments of my soul."

- **Visualisation:** Imagine yourself walking through a serene landscape, such as a rainforest, a coastline, or a realm of pure light. Envision glowing lights that represent the aspects of yourself that remain tied to the original traumatic event.

- **Integration:** Gently gather these lights, send compassion and understanding to these reclaimed parts welcoming them back home into your heart energy centre, or a dedicated energetic space.
- **Breathe** deeply as you feel these reclaimed fragments reintegrating into your being.
- **Gratitude:** Conclude by expressing gratitude for your willingness to heal and for the aspects of yourself that have been returned.

Energy Centre Meditation

- **Grounding:** Begin by visualising the Earth Star Chakra beneath your feet, connecting you to Earth's core. Breathe in grounding energy, stabilising your subtle body.
- **Ascending Through Centers:** Move upward through the root, sacral, solar plexus, heart, throat, third eye, and crown chakras, pausing at each to invite clearing and healing.
- **Higher Chakras:** Expand your focus to the Soul Star Chakra above your head, inviting higher wisdom and cosmic perspective. Take a moment to feel the alignment and flow from Earth Star to Soul Star.
- **Completion:** Bring your awareness back to your heart centre. Express gratitude for this synergy of energies and anchor the experience by imagining roots growing from your feet into the Earth, securing your newfound balance.

Journaling Prompts

- **Fragmented Aspects:** What areas of your life feel fragmented or incomplete? Reflect on possible energetic events (traumatic or otherwise) that may have contributed to these feelings.

- **Emotional Gateways:** Recall a challenging emotion you've experienced recently. What message might it hold regarding your energetic state?

- **Recurring Patterns:** Identify a recurring relational or behavioural pattern in your life. How could it be tied to unresolved energy from a past event?

- **Higher Self Connection:** Write about any synchronicities or intuitive nudges that appear when you explore your trauma through an energetic lens.

CHAPTER 4:
The Cosmic Soul

The soul of a star being is often referred to as a Cosmic Soul, one which embodies unity consciousness, contrasting with the duality and separation often felt on Earth, in the third dimension. This unity consciousness is anchored in love, compassion, and the realisation that all beings are interconnected. This interconnectedness reflects the ancient thought systems that posit nothing exists in isolation.

The Cosmic Soul can be understood as the vast, interconnected extension of the individuated universal self, a greater consciousness that exists both within and beyond the individual. Representing a profound and intricate relationship between the physical, emotional, and spiritual dimensions.

This chapter explores the profound unity between human existence and the higher, cosmic essence of the Divine. Explored, is the Cosmic Soul as a vast, interconnected aspect of our being that exists beyond physical limitations. In turn, the Cosmic Soul links us to unity consciousness and the broader cosmos.

The pages following explains how we are essentially star beings with cosmic DNA. Further, that we are capable of accessing higher dimensions of consciousness through the development of our light body. Also, through the activation of chakras beyond the traditional seven.

Through understanding and integrating this cosmic nature, we learn to move beyond the illusion of separation and embrace our role in the collective evolution of consciousness, all while anchoring these higher awareness states into our daily lives on Earth. The soul is not bound to the physical realm but is a manifestation of the cosmos within us, traversing multiple planes of reality.

By recognising this connection, we come to understand that our souls are eternal, transcendent entities, continuously evolving within this cosmos and expanding beyond the limitations of the material world. By engaging with this cosmic connection, we begin to understand that our souls are not limited to earthly experiences but are entities that traverse multiple planes of reality.

The concept of the soul possessing a cosmic set of DNA codes activated within us implies that we can access new centres of consciousness. This understanding rests on the principle that the soul holds a cosmic body—one that has lived more lives as a celestial or star being than as a human. Through accessing the Cosmic Soul, one transcends the limitations of 5D density, connecting with the broader planetary and cosmic forces that shape our identity as star beings.

Understanding the Cosmic Soul

The concept of the Cosmic Soul invites us to see ourselves

as more than just physical beings. Rather, we can envision ourselves as energetic beings with roots in multiple star systems. Being a sentient being from these star systems you would often be referred to as Starseeds. Starseed soul carries the imprint of experiences from other dimensions and planets, bringing knowledge, wisdom, and a unique energetic signature to Earth. However, the Starseeds we are bonded with feel a deep resonance with the cosmos, and often experience a longing for "home." Home being in the higher dimensional realms.

Each aspect of reality is a thread in a vast cosmic web, linking everything from the smallest atom to the largest star system. Ancient traditions, whose practices are embedded in our DNA, stipulate that our interactions with ourselves, others, and our environments, affects entire systems. Quantum physics echoes this principle known as entanglement in which particles are described as related and affecting each other across vast distances, reinforcing the notion that separation is an illusion.

As we awaken to our cosmic nature, we begin to dissolve the barriers that confine us to limited perceptions of self, opening pathways to higher states of awareness. Recognising the interconnected web of life invites a greater sense of responsibility and compassion for all beings. We begin to realise that by tending to our personal healing, we can participate in the healing of others and the cosmos at large.

Spiritual Evolution & the Cosmic Soul

Integration is the process of harmonising the insights, lessons, and fragmented aspects of the self that arise during spiritual growth. As we navigate emotional healing, soul retrieval, and alignment with the Higher Self, integration ensures that these experiences contribute to lasting transformation. Without integration, spiritual breakthroughs risk becoming fleeting moments, rather than catalysts for long-term change.

To fully integrate the Cosmic Soul, one must consistently reflect, engage in grounding practices, and apply newfound awareness to daily life. This is not about attaining perfection, rather, it's about embracing a state of continual growth and self-awareness. The process highlights the dance between the physical and spiritual realms, emphasising that both are essential to the human experience.

Cosmic Soul & the Light Body

The Cosmic Soul perspective expands this to include fifteen chakras existing across multiple dimensions. Chakras eight through fifteen connect us to higher states of consciousness and facilitate the integration of the light body. This is the energetic counterpart to our physical form.

- **Chakras 8-12:** Represent higher spiritual awareness and bridge the physical body to the light body.
- **Chakras 13-15:** Align with universal consciousness, connecting us to divine intelligence and cosmic forces.

Developing the light body is essential for expanding beyond the limitations of the third-dimensional (Earth) experience. By doing so we are able to access higher realms of consciousness. Cultivation of the light body enhances our intuitive abilities, accelerating healing processes, and creating stronger alignments with our Higher Self.

Embracing the Spiral Path

Spiritual growth is not linear but follows a spiral path, where lessons revisit us at deeper levels over time. Embracing this spiral journey allows for greater self-compassion, as it acknowledges that growth often involves revisiting old wounds, patterns, or beliefs from new perspectives.

The spiral path invites humility and patience, reminding us that each cycle of growth offers new insights and opportunities for healing. By honouring this cyclical process, we align more deeply with the rhythms of the universe.

The Power of a Community of Healing

As each person aligns with their Cosmic Soul, their healing ripples outward, influencing families, communities, and the broader collective consciousness. This ripple effect underscores the interconnected nature of reality; where individual growth contributes to the evolution of humanity as a whole.

A community of healing emerges when groups of people engage in practices that practice inter-connectedness, compassion, and mutual support. This can take the form of community meditation circles, collaborative healing sessions, or group rituals dedicated to planetary well-being, known as gridwork.

Anchoring the Cosmic Soul in Daily Life

Living with the awareness of the Cosmic Soul is a practice of embodying higher consciousness in everyday experiences. It is manifesting the divine through the mundane. It calls for presence, compassion, and the courage to embrace both the light and shadow within. By integrating spiritual insights, nurturing multidimensional awareness, and contributing to collective healing, we step fully into our role as co-creators of a more harmonious reality.

This journey is one of continuous unfolding, where each step reveals deeper aspects of our true nature. As we align with the Cosmic Soul, we illuminate not only our path, but also the paths of those around us. This can foster a shared journey toward greater unity and enlightenment.

The Cosmic Soul can be seen as the Divine, universal essence within each individual that transcends personal identity, linking us directly to the grand design of the cosmos.

By embracing a spectrum of practices, ranging from meditation, sound healing, and astrology to esoteric philosophies, energy work, and community based teachings, such as those we provide at *TheMultidimensionalSoul.com* - seekers can cultivate an ever-closer relationship with this higher dimension of self.

The journey of discovering and aligning with the cosmic soul is intensely personal. Yet, a person can be enriched by the wisdom of those who have walked the path before. In this exploration, each new insight and experience serves to deepen understanding, and also to reaffirm the profound unity that underlies all existence.

Embodying the Cosmic Soul does not imply detachment from everyday life; rather, it encourages approaching daily experiences with a heightened sense of wonder, purpose, and interconnectedness.

Whether through quiet moments of meditation, the echo of a sacred chant, or the illumination of divine guidance, the cosmic soul beckons. Consider incorporating daily practices to help remind you that we are all inextricably woven into the fabric of creation.

By accepting this sacred invitation, you too can discover that life on Earth is a canvas for infinite exploration and self-realisation. With the cosmos as guide and companion.

What's Next?

In the next chapter, you will dive into the multidimensional nature of the soul, exploring how it exists beyond the boundaries of space and time.

We'll discover how our consciousness weaves through parallel realities, different timelines, and various dimensions, creating a rich tapestry of experience and growth. By understanding this vast aspect of ourselves, we begin to grasp not only our infinite potential but also how we can integrate these multiple layers of being into our everyday lives, transforming our perspective of reality and our place within it.

Meanwhile, to review and conceptualise the learnings in Chapter 4, a set of activities follows for you to complete at your own pace.

Shadow Work Journaling

Reflect on recent instances of anger or frustration and ask yourself:
- What triggered this emotion?
- How does this reflect unmet needs or boundaries?
- What lessons can be drawn from this experience?

- How can I cultivate a balanced perspective without dismissing my feelings?

Journaling Synchronicities and Growth Toward Ascension

Reflecting on your spiritual journey can reveal insights and highlight growth that may otherwise go unnoticed. Use this journaling activity to track synchronicities, shifts in patterns, and moments of clarity that align with your soul's evolution:

- **Synchronicities:** Write about recent experiences where meaningful coincidences occurred. How did they relate to your current path?
- **Negative Patterns Dissolving:** Reflect on any recurring negative patterns that have lessened or disappeared. What changes in your behaviour or mindset contributed to this shift?
- **Harmony in Relationships:** Note any improvements in personal or professional relationships. How do these reflect your inner growth and evolving energy?
- **Soul's Purpose Clarity:** Describe moments of insight or clarity regarding your soul's purpose. What experiences or realisations led to these moments?

Integration Reflection

- Reflect on a recent spiritual insight or emotional breakthrough. How can you apply this awareness in your daily life?
- Journal about moments where you felt alignment with your Higher Self. What shifts occurred in your thoughts or behaviors?

- Identify areas where further integration is needed. How can you nurture this process?

Community of Healing Meditation

- Visualise yourself as part of a vast web of light, connecting with others across the globe.
- Send intentions of healing, love, and peace outward, imagining them flowing through this web.
- Reflect on how your personal healing contributes to this collective energy.

Spiral Reflection

- Reflect on a recurring challenge in your life. How has your relationship to this challenge evolved over time?
- What new lessons are emerging from revisiting this aspect of your journey?
- Celebrate the growth that has occurred, even if the journey feels incomplete.
- Consider planting a small section of your yard or patio to aid connection with the cyclical patterns of life.

CHAPTER 5:
The Multidimensional Soul: Beyond Space and Time

Understanding the Essence of Who You Are

Embodying the Cosmic Soul means embracing ourselves as multidimensional beings. As such, capable of experiencing and interacting with various planes of existence. This understanding invites us to live with greater purpose, aligning our actions with our higher calling. It challenges us to honour the energetic connection between ourselves, each other, the broader planet, and the vast cosmos.

Living multidimensionally does not require abandoning the material. Rather, it is a call for a balanced approach to lifestyle choices, where spiritual insights inform practical decisions. This balance cultivates a sense of unity between the inner and outer worlds, allowing us to navigate challenges with grace and resilience.

The light body acts as a vehicle for multidimensional travel, allowing us to bridge gaps between different realities and gain insights from higher frequencies. This development not only nurtures personal growth but also strengthens our ability to serve as conduits of light. This enhances the elevation of human consciousness as a whole. As our light body evolves, our capacity to manifest, heal, and co-create with the universe intensifies, reflecting the interconnected nature of existence.

Soul Incarnation into Physical Form

Each incarnation is a different hue, a unique expression of the same eternal source. From a multidimensional perspective, incarnation serves as a classroom for growth. The dense and often challenging nature of Earth offers experiences that other realms cannot provide. Conflict, love, loss, and rebirth catalyse soul expansion.

However, incarnation comes with a price, the Veil of Forgetfulness. When the soul enters the body, it forgets its divine origins to fully immerse in the human experience. This veil is not a punishment but a gift. Through forgetting, the soul rediscovers itself anew, allowing for profound growth and mastery.

Living Beyond the Physical

Recognising that you are more than your body reshapes how you live. Decisions are no longer based solely on material concerns, rather they align with your soul's greater mission. Relationships shift as you seek those who resonate with your higher frequency. Even day-to-day struggles take on new meaning when viewed through the lens of soul growth.

Living as a multidimensional being means understanding that every interaction, every experience, echoes across lifetimes and dimensions. Each act of love, compassion, or forgiveness sends ripples through the cosmos, influencing not just your path but the paths of countless others.

As we continue this journey through the pages ahead, we will explore the nature of reality, the chakras as portals, Earth's awakening process, and the role of cosmic beings in humanity's evolution. But first, take a moment to reflect on this truth:

> *You are eternal. You are vast. You are the universe experiencing itself through human form.*

Signs of the Multidimensional Soul in Daily Life

Even with the veil in place, glimpses of the soul's vastness breakthrough in subtle yet powerful ways.

Déjà vu – A fleeting sense that you've been somewhere before, likely a memory from a parallel life or timeline.

Vivid Dreams – Dreams that feel more real than waking life, suggesting astral travel or interaction with higher dimensions.

Out-of-Body Experiences (OBEs) – Moments when your consciousness lifts from the body, traveling through other realms.

Sudden Epiphanies – Flashes of insight or wisdom that seem to come from nowhere, often messages from the higher self.

Synchronicities – Repeated patterns or meaningful coincidences that point to higher guidance at work.

Remembering Who We Are

Awakening is the moment the soul begins to remember; an unravelling of the Veil of Forgetting that reconnects the person with their multidimensional essence. It is a return to the truth of our cosmic origins, the realisation that we are not merely physical beings bound by time, but luminous souls existing across parallel dimensions.

The awakening process is not a single event but a gradual unfolding, often catalysed by life's challenges, synchronicities, or sudden spiritual revelations.

While awakening may seem spontaneous, it is often triggered by life's transformative moments:

- **Loss or Trauma** – The shattering of the ego through grief, illness, or hardship.

- **Sudden Joy or Love** – Deep experiences of connection, such as the birth of a child or the experience of unconditional love.

- **Near-Death Experiences (NDEs)** – Encounters with the soul's existence beyond the body.

- **Spiritual Practices** – Meditation, yoga, breathwork, or energy healing that elevates consciousness.

- Moments of profound peace and connection with the Earth.

For many, the awakening process begins subtly, a series of nudges from the universe, gradually building until the soul can no longer ignore the call.

Signs of Lightbody Activation include:

- Intense tingling or vibrations in the body.
- Seeing geometric patterns or light codes during meditation.
- Increased awareness of energy fields and auras.
- Spontaneous heart openings or waves of love.

The awakening process is not a destination but an ongoing journey, a dance between forgetting and remembering. Each moment of expansion ripples across timelines, contributing to the collective shift of humanity and Earth.

The Quantum Nature of Reality

Modern science offers glimpses into this multidimensional landscape. The field of quantum mechanics reveals that particles can exist in multiple states at once, a phenomenon known as superposition.

Similarly, the observer effect shows that reality shifts based on the observer's focus and intention. This implies that consciousness plays a pivotal role in shaping the fabric of reality.

If subatomic particles respond to consciousness, then reality at large must operate by the same principles. The world we perceive is not fixed but fluid, bending and shifting according to our vibrational state and awareness.

Dreams and Astral Travel: Gateways to Parallel Dimensions

One of the most direct ways we access parallel realities is through dreams.

Have you ever awakened from a dream so vivid it felt more real than waking life? These experiences are not mere figments of imagination but journeys into alternate dimensions.

- **Lucid dreams** often reveal alternate versions of yourself—living in different timelines, interacting with unfamiliar yet familiar faces.
- **Astral travel** allows the conscious soul to leave the body and explore higher realms, moving freely through different layers of existence.

In these states, the veil between dimensions thins, allowing your soul to experience the multidimensional landscape firsthand.

The Illusion of Separation and Time

From birth, many of us are socialised to view life as a linear progression, a journey from past to present to future. This perception anchors us in the third-dimensional (3D) reality of physicality, where cause and effect govern our experiences.

Yet, quantum physics and ancient spiritual traditions converge on one profound truth: *time is not linear.*

Time is more accurately described as a spiral, a loop, or even a field where past, present, and future coexist simultaneously. The multidimensional soul perceives this fluidity intuitively. When you experience déjà vu, precognitive dreams, or sudden flashes of past lives, you are temporarily stepping beyond the illusion of time, accessing parallel versions of reality.

Linear time exists only in the 3D realm, a construct

designed for structured learning and soul growth. In higher dimensions, time behaves differently:

- **In the fourth dimension (4D)**, time becomes more malleable, allowing glimpses of alternate futures or the ability to revisit the past.

- **In the fifth dimension (5D)** and beyond, time dissolves entirely. All possibilities exist simultaneously, and the soul operates from a state of eternal "now."

Parallel Realities: Infinite Versions of You

One of the most fascinating aspects of multidimensionality is the existence of parallel realities.

Imagine standing at a crossroads. Each direction represents a different decision, leading to alternate outcomes. In the physical world, you choose one path, but in the quantum field, every path is taken.

Parallel realities are not distant or inaccessible; they unfold alongside this one, separated only by the frequency of your consciousness. Your soul exists across these timelines, experiencing various lives, lessons, and possibilities all at once.

- In one reality, you may have pursued a different career.
- In another, you live in a different part of the world.
- In some realities, subtle differences unfold, while in others, the shifts are monumental.

These parallel selves are not distant strangers; they are you, fragments of your multidimensional soul exploring the infinite potential of existence.

Breaking Free from Linear Time

Reality is not as rigid as it appears. The world around us, solid, tangible, and bound by linear time, is only a fragment of a much larger, multidimensional existence. Beneath the surface of our waking life lies a vast network of parallel realities, each vibrating at different frequencies yet coexisting within the same cosmic fabric.

The multidimensional soul navigates these realities fluidly, transcending the constraints of space and time. In this chapter, we delve into the true nature of reality, exploring the hidden realms where the soul resides and the infinite possibilities that unfold when we break free from the illusion of linearity.

The Ripple Effect: How Choices Shape Reality

Every thought, action, and decision create ripples across the quantum field, influencing not only this reality but countless parallel timelines. This is known as the ripple effect.

For example:
- When you choose forgiveness over resentment, you shift the energy of not just your life but the collective field of humanity.
- Acts of kindness in one timeline may inspire healing in another.

The interconnectedness of realities means that growth in one dimension accelerates the evolution of the entire soul across all timelines.

Merging Timelines: Integrating the Self

One of the ultimate goals of the multidimensional journey

is to merge fragmented aspects of the self across parallel dimensions.

Through deep meditation, soul retrieval practices, and conscious intention, you can call forth these versions of yourself, integrating their lessons and gifts into this present reality. This process accelerates spiritual growth, leading to profound healing and greater alignment with your higher self.

Pathways to Higher Realms

The chakras, as discussed previously, are more than energy centers, they are cosmic portals, linking the physical body to higher dimensions of existence. As conduits of divine energy, chakras regulate the flow of consciousness between the material and spiritual realms. When fully activated, they allow the soul to transcend 3D limitations and access the vast landscape of parallel dimensions, guiding the path of ascension.

Beyond the seven physical chakras lie morphogenic chakras, higher energetic centers that connect to the cosmic planes of reality. These chakras are not limited to the physical body but extend into etheric, astral, and celestial dimensions.

Multidimensional Chakras and Emotional Healing

Expanding upon the traditional understanding of our energy centers, spiritual teacher Lisa Renee emphasise the Ayurvedic multidimensional perspective, to include higher chakras. These additional energy centers connect us to greater aspects of consciousness and facilitate deeper emotional healing.

The 8th Chakra (Soul Star) connects us to the Higher Self and our soul's purpose, while the 9th Chakra (Spirit Chakra) accesses collective consciousness and spiritual gifts. Additionally, Chakras 10 through 12 link us to cosmic consciousness and unity with the divine. By integrating these higher energy centers, we can access profound levels of healing and awareness of our potential and purpose.

Emotional healing involves reclaiming fragmented aspects of the soul across different timelines and dimensions. Practices such as soul fragment retrieval, auric clearing, and holographic healing, address imbalances in the multidimensional layers of the energy body. This can restore our integrity and unity as an energetic being having a human experience.

In total, spiritual teachings identify 15 primary chakras spread across different layers of the multidimensional self:

1. **Root** (Muladhara) – Grounding in the physical world (3D).
2. **Sacral** (Svadhisthana) – Emotional flow and creativity (3D).
3. **Solar Plexus** (Manipura) – Personal power and identity (3D).
4. **Heart** (Anahata) – Love and unity (4D, gateway to higher realms).
5. **Throat** (Vishuddha) – Expression and truth (5D).
6. **Third Eye** (Ajna) – Intuition and foresight (6D).
7. **Crown** (Sahasrara) – Connection to Source (7D).
8. **Soul Star Chakra** – Access to soul contracts and Akashic records (8D).
9. **Galactic Chakra** – Connection to cosmic energies (9D).

10. **Universal Chakra** – Union with collective consciousness (10D).
11. **Earth Star Chakra** – Anchoring divine energy into Earth (11D).
12. **Stellar Gateway** – Portal to higher star systems (12D).
13. **Cosmic Gateway** – Access to intergalactic dimensions (13D).
14. **Ascension Chakra** – Full embodiment of divine light (14D).
15. **The Core Star Chakra** – Connection to the Source beyond creation (15D).

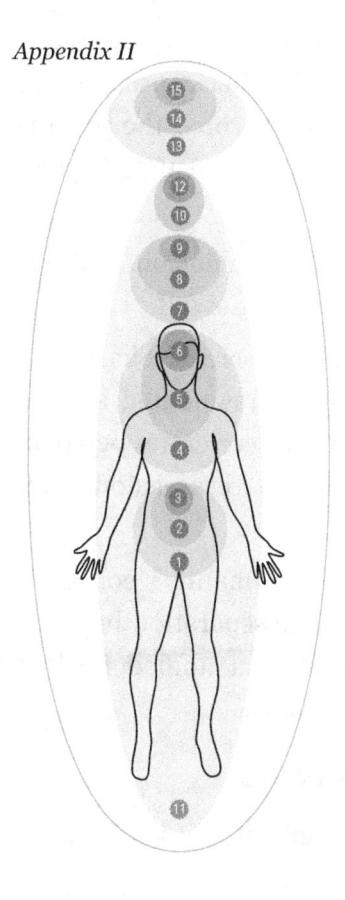

Appendix II

15 CHAKRAS

1 : Root
2 : Sacral
3 : Solar Plexus
4 : Heart
5 : Throat
6 : Third Eye
7 : Crown
8 : Soul Star Chakra
9 : Galactic Chakra
10: Universal Chakra
11: Earth Star Chakra
12: Stella Gateway
13: Cosmic Gateway
14: Ascension Chakra
15: The Core Star Chakra

In 3D existence, chakras appear as cone-like vortexes that pull in energy. However, as the soul ascends into higher states, the chakras evolve into cylindrical tunnels of light, dynamic, ever-flowing pathways that merge with the holographic anatomy of the soul.

- In 3D reality, chakras are individual, functioning separately to sustain physical life.
- In 5D and beyond, the chakras merge into one unified stream of energy, flowing effortlessly between dimensions. This is often referred to as the activation of the light body.

This transformation dissolves crystalline seals, energetic barriers preventing the free flow of higher consciousness into the physical body. As these seals dissolve, the chakras become stargates, connecting the soul to realms beyond linear time.

Each chakra not only connects to a dimension but also serves as a portal to parallel versions of the self.

When the chakras are in alignment, they create a harmonic resonance across timelines, allowing fragmented aspects of the soul to reunite. This integration accelerates personal growth, empowering the individual to access wisdom from all parallel selves.

As Earth transitions from 3D to 5D, humanity's collective chakra system mirrors this shift. The separation between individual chakras dissolves, creating a unified field of energy. Duality fades and unity prevails.

Fragments of Light and the Whole

As the soul is not a singular, isolated entity it is of benefit to learn about it as a holographic fragment of the universe itself. Just as a hologram contains the entire image within each part, the soul carries the full imprint of Source energy, existing simultaneously across dimensions and timelines. This understanding reshapes how we view existence, revealing that we are not bound by physical form but woven into the vast, interconnected tapestry of creation.

The Holographic Principle: As Above, So Below

Ancient spiritual traditions and modern physics converge on one profound truth: the universe is holographic. The principle "as above, so below" reflects this reality, what exists on the micro level mirrors the macro.

In a hologram, the whole image is encoded within every part. Similarly, each fragment of our soul contains the full essence of who we are. This means that:

- Your higher self exists in each moment of your life.
- Every experience reflects the broader cosmic journey of your soul.
- Healing one aspect of your consciousness influences and heals parallel versions of yourself across dimensions.

The soul functions as a fractal, a self-replicating pattern that expands infinitely while maintaining its core design. Each incarnation, lifetime, or dimension the soul inhabits is a smaller reflection of the greater whole.

This fractal nature means the soul exists in:

- **Multiple Timelines** – Alternate realities where different choices have unfolded.

- **Higher Dimensions** – Aspects of the self that operate beyond the limits of 3D consciousness.

- **Parallel Lives** – Simultaneous incarnations of the same soul in different forms and realms.

The holographic soul expresses itself through stations of identity or energetic nodes representing different facets of who we are across time and space. Each station serves as a checkpoint in the soul's evolution, reflecting growth, lessons, and experiences.

For example:

- A version of you in a past life as a healer may still influence your current abilities.
- A parallel self, existing in a more advanced timeline may offer insight and guidance during meditation.
- Future versions of your soul may assist in guiding present decisions.

These identities are not separate but interconnected, forming a web of consciousness that spans the universe.

Holographic Healing and Integration

One of the most powerful aspects of the holographic model is the ability to heal and integrate across timelines. When we address wounds or patterns in this life, the effects ripple across parallel realities, creating shifts throughout the entire soul matrix.

Healing Techniques:

1. **Quantum Healing** – Accessing parallel versions of the self through meditation or hypnotherapy.

2. **Timeline Integration** – Visualising fractured parts of the soul returning to the present self.
3. **Inner Child Work** – Healing younger versions of the self to release present emotional blocks.

Exercise: Recalling Holographic Fragments

This exercise helps you tap into the holographic aspects of your soul, allowing you to connect with other versions of yourself.

1. Sit quietly and center your breathing.
2. Visualise a mirror in front of you. As you gaze into it, ask to see a version of yourself that holds wisdom or healing you need at this moment.
3. Allow an image to form. Observe the clothing, surroundings, and energy of this parallel self.
4. Ask them to step forward, merging into your present form.
5. Feel the integration of their knowledge and light into your being.
6. Express gratitude and return to the present moment.

The Role of the Akashic Records

The Akashic Records are believed to be a holographic database of every thought, action, and experience throughout the soul's journey. This cosmic library holds the key to understanding your multidimensional self, offering insight into past lives, parallel realities, and future potentials.

Through deep meditation or working with Akashic record

keepers, you can access these records, uncovering the root causes of current life patterns and dissolving blockages across timelines.

How to Access the Akashic Records:

- Enter meditation and visualise ascending a spiral staircase or entering a grand library.
- Ask to access the record of your soul's blueprint.
- Pay attention to symbols, images, or messages that emerge.
- Record any insights upon returning to waking consciousness.

The soul learns through repeating patterns, revisiting the same lessons across different lifetimes and dimensions. This cyclical nature is not punishment but an opportunity for growth and mastery.

When a lesson is fully integrated, the karmic cycle dissolves, allowing the soul to progress to higher states of being.

To embody the holographic soul is to live with the awareness that every thought, word, and action ripples through the cosmos.

Practical ways to embrace this include:

- **Mindfulness** – Cultivating present awareness, knowing each moment shapes alternate realities.
- **Service to Others** – Recognising that by uplifting others, you heal aspects of yourself across dimensions.
- **Gratitude and Forgiveness** – Energetic tools that dissolve karmic patterns and restore harmony to the holographic field.

Ascension: From Duality to Unity

Humanity stands at the precipice of a profound transformation, the ascension from 3D duality to 5D unity consciousness. This evolutionary leap is not only an expansion of individual awareness but a collective shift, guided by cosmic forces and Earth's rising vibration. At the heart of this process lies the embodiment of unconditional love, divine unity, and the realisation that separation is an illusion.

As a reminder, ascension is the process by which the soul, individually and collectively, raises its vibrational frequency, transitioning from the dense experience of 3D to higher-dimensional states. It is often described as moving from fear-based separation to love-based unity.

In essence, ascension is a return to our divine origins, where the soul fully remembers its interconnectedness with all beings, the cosmos, and Source itself.

Key Aspects of Ascension

- **Shift in Consciousness** – Moving from ego-driven reality to heart-centered living.
- **Physical Evolution** – Activation of the light body, allowing the human form to hold more light and higher frequencies.
- **Emotional Healing** – Releasing dense karmic imprints, traumas, and ancestral wounds.
- **Awakening of Gifts** – Heightened psychic abilities, telepathy, and multidimensional perception.

Humanity's current existence in 3D is characterised by

duality, conflict, and the belief in separation. In 5D, these divisions dissolve, replaced by oneness, peace, and higher awareness.

As the physical and energetic bodies adjust to higher frequencies, many experience ascension symptoms. These are signs of the body recalibrating, shedding lower densities, and activating dormant DNA.

Common Ascension Symptoms

- **Physical:** Fatigue, dizziness, body aches, headaches, and light sensitivity.
- **Emotional:** Unexplained grief, sudden joy, or emotional purging.
- **Mental:** Heightened intuition, racing thoughts, or vivid downloads of information.
- **Spiritual:** Stronger connection to guides, increased synchronicities, and lucid dreams.

The Crystalline Grid

Earth's energetic anatomy mirrors the awakening of humanity. Surrounding the planet is a crystalline grid, an energetic web of light that holds the blueprint for unconditional love and unity of the cosmos.

This grid is activated through more souls awakening to their divine nature, and contributing light to this grid, accelerating the ascension process for all.

Though ascension begins at the individual level, it is ultimately a collective phenomenon. As more souls awaken, the vibratory threshold of Earth rises, creating ripples throughout the galactic network.

Every act of love, forgiveness, and compassion contributes to the collective ascension.

Conclusion - A Multidimensional Playground

The nature of reality is far more expansive than we can comprehend. As multidimensional beings, we are constantly weaving through infinite timelines, learning, growing, and evolving across the vast cosmic tapestry.

By expanding our awareness beyond the constraints of linear time, we unlock the full potential of the soul, accessing parallel lives, dissolving the illusion of separation, and embracing the truth that all is connected.

The chakras are not mere spiritual concepts; they are the soul's cosmic compass, guiding us through realms seen and unseen. By understanding and activating these gateways, we unlock the full potential of our multidimensional existence.

In the next chapter, we will explore Earth's Ascension Process and how the planet's evolving energy fields mirror our spiritual growth.

The holographic nature of the soul reveals that we are not separate from the universe, we are reflections of its infinite light. By embracing this understanding, we unlock the potential to heal, expand, and embody the fullness of our multidimensional being.

Ascension and the awakening of unity in unconditional love represent the next step in humanity's evolution. This journey is not about escaping the physical but integrating higher frequencies into the body, mind, and spirit. We become conduits for divine love, transforming not only our lives but the world around us.

A Living, Evolving Consciousness

Earth is far more than a physical planet; it is a sentient being undergoing its own evolutionary journey. Just as humanity ascends in consciousness, Earth too shifts, rising through dimensional layers in a process often referred to as planetary ascension. This mutual evolution intertwines human souls with the planet, creating a profound symbiotic relationship that influences the collective awakening.

For centuries, Indigenous cultures and ancient civilisations have recognised Earth as a living entity. Known by many names, Gaia, Pachamama, Terra, she is revered as the Great Mother, a nurturing force that sustains all life.

From a multidimensional perspective, Earth exists across multiple planes of reality, just as we do. Her physical body (the 3D world we experience) is mirrored by etheric, astral, and higher-dimensional layers. These layers vibrate at frequencies that align with the chakra system of the planet.

- **1D-3D** – Earth's physical form and mineral kingdom.
- **4D** – The emotional layer, where collective consciousness and thought forms reside.
- **5D** – The heart of Gaia, a realm of unity consciousness.
- **6D-12D** – Cosmic layers connecting Earth to galactic grids and universal intelligence.

Earth's ascension process involves raising the vibratory rate of her physical and energetic bodies, allowing her to transition from 3D duality to 5D unity. This shift reflects the collective evolution of humanity, as both beings ascend in harmony.

Human souls and Earth share a deeply interconnected journey. Every thought, emotion, and action we project influences Earth's energetic field. In turn, Earth's vibratory shifts affect our personal and collective growth.

Earth's Ascension Timeline

Earth's ascension is not sudden; it unfolds over thousands of years in alignment with cosmic cycles. Ancient cultures, such as the Maya and Egyptians, tracked these cycles through calendars and monuments aligned with celestial bodies.

One of the most significant milestones in this timeline is the transition from the Piscean Age (3D consciousness) to the Aquarian Age (5D consciousness). This shift signifies humanity's movement toward enlightenment, cooperation, and spiritual remembrance.

The Magnetic Field and Earth's Lightbody

Earth's magnetic field is more than a shield against cosmic radiation; it is part of her light body. This energetic grid functions like the human aura, regulating planetary health and maintaining balance.

As Earth ascends, this field undergoes geomagnetic shifts, reflecting the planet's rising frequency. Many people sensitive to energy experience these shifts physically, manifesting as:

- Fatigue or dizziness during solar flares.
- Vivid dreams and astral experiences.
- Increased empathy and emotional release.

The thinning of Earth's magnetic field allows for

greater interaction between dimensions, facilitating communication with higher realms.

The surface of Earth is crisscrossed by ley lines which are energetic highways that link sacred sites and power points. At the intersections of these lines are stargates—portals to higher dimensions.

These stargates are activated during specific alignments, such as eclipses, solstices, and equinoxes, allowing cosmic energy to infuse the planet. When large groups meditate or gather at these points, the energy amplifies, accelerating both personal and planetary ascension.

Humanity's Collective Role in Earth's Ascension

Every soul incarnated at this time contributes to the ascension process. Whether through personal healing, environmental stewardship, or spiritual practice, each individual anchors light into the collective field.

Simple acts of love, forgiveness, and compassion ripple across dimensions, elevating Earth's frequency. Meditation, grounding, and connecting to nature are powerful tools that synchronise personal vibration with the planet's ascension.

Multidimensional Chakra Meditation

Begin by finding a quiet, comfortable space where you won't be disturbed. Using *Appendix II*, ground yourself by visualising roots extending from your Earth Star chakra, deep into the Earth, anchoring you firmly. Then, starting with the Earth Star Chakra, which is 6 inches below your feet, aim to activate it through awareness of it. Slowly progress upward through the traditional chakras toward the Stellar Gateway Chakra in the solar system surrounding earth. Visualise each chakra as a radiant sphere of light, expanding and harmonising. Set the intention to heal emotionally within this chakra, allowing healing energy to flow through you, restoring balance and unity to your conscious self.

Practical Steps to Embody Multidimensional Awareness

1. **Grounding Rituals:** Engage in daily practices that anchor your energy, such as walking in nature, breathwork, or mindful movement.
2. **Spiritual Hygiene:** Regularly clear your energy through meditation, visualisation, or sound healing.
3. **Service and Compassion:** Act in ways that uplift others, understanding that service reflects cosmic interconnectedness.
4. **Creative Expression:** Use art, music, dance or writing for example, to channel and express your multidimensional experiences.

Visit our YouTube channel:
@themultidimensionalsoul1292 for free meditations to support you on your spiritual awakening journey.

Or visit our website, **TheMultidimensionalSoul.com** where you will find many of the meditations in this book. We are always adding to our library of videos!

CHAPTER 6:
Resources to Develop the Multidimensional Soul

An array of literature exists to provide you with indepth explorations of the soul, offering theoretical insights and practical exercises.

This chapter provides a comprehensive resource guide for developing and exploring the multidimensional soul and concepts and practices from the other chapters. The list covers key texts, spiritual practices, and practical techniques.

The chapter encompasses both ancient wisdom traditions and modern approaches, offering readers multiple pathways to deepen their spiritual connection and understanding of their cosmic nature through practices that range from simple daily rituals to advanced metaphysical techniques.

These texts can guide you to a richer connection with your divine essence. Cultivating the awareness that your soul allows for transcendence of everyday consciousness.

THE COSMIC GAME: Explorations of the Frontiers of Human Consciousness, by Stanislav Grof.

Stanislav Grof, a luminary in transpersonal psychology. He investigates the nature of higher consciousness and cosmic awareness through pioneering research into altered states of consciousness.

Integrating scientific methodologies with spiritual inquiry, Grof's work underscores how experiences in non-ordinary reality can reveal the interconnectedness of the soul and the universe.

Readers seeking to explore the cosmic dimension of their being will find his analyses of near-death experiences, psychedelic therapy, and holotropic breathwork, invaluable tools for expanding awareness.

THE POWER OF NOW by Eckhart Tolle

Eckhart Tolle's groundbreaking book underscores the importance of living in the present moment as a pathway to spiritual insight. By practicing mindfulness and stillness, a person can tap into their cosmic soul and perceive how their daily life is woven into a larger cosmic canvas.

Tolle's emphasis on transcending the "mind's chatter" to reconnect with the stillness within, resonates for those seeking a direct experience of their divine nature.

THE TIBETAN BOOK OF LIVING AND DYING by Sogyal Rinpoche

Based on Tibetan Buddhist teachings, this text explores the nature of the soul through the lens of reincarnation, impermanence, and spiritual liberation. The work highlights how the soul essence navigates the cycle of birth, death, and rebirth, underscoring themes of cosmic unity and divine awareness.

Through contemplative practices, readers are guided to experience their interconnectedness with all of existence.

Journey of Souls by Michael Newton offers case studies of past-life regression and between-life experiences, shedding light on the soul's cosmic trajectory and purpose.

WORKS BY PARAMAHANSA YOGANANDA (e.g., Autobiography of a Yogi)

Explore states of divine realisation and cosmic consciousness, providing personal testimony and practical guidance.

SPIRITUAL PRACTICES

A variety of spiritual practices support you to connect with your soul, promoting heightened awareness of divine consciousness and the higher planes of existence.

Meditation and Deep Contemplation

Meditation forms the foundation for cultivating an awareness of the divine self. Techniques such as transcendental meditation, Vipassana, mantra meditation, and self inquiry can quieten the mind, unveiling layers of consciousness that often remain hidden in daily life.

Through committed practice you may encounter glimpses of your cosmic soul, and realise the sacred spark within that resonates with universal oneness.

Astral Projection and Out-of-Body Experiences (OBEs)

Methods for astral projection, made famous by Robert Monroe's Journeys Out of the Body, involve transcending the perceived limits of the physical form to explore subtler realms.

Many practitioners report encounters with celestial guides and divine energies during OBEs, contributing to a greater understanding of the cosmic soul and its place in the grand universal design.

Channelling and Spiritual Mediumship

For those inclined to explore communication with higher energies, channelling offers a pathway to directly receive messages from celestial guides or one's own higher self.

Resources like Opening to Channel by Sanaya Roman provide practical steps for safely and ethically engaging with these energies. Such practices aim to sharpen intuition and strengthen the individual's connection to cosmic consciousness.

Shamanic Journeys

Facilitated by drumming or plant medicine (where legal and culturally appropriate), these experiences can lead to profound insights into the soul's multidimensional nature.

Prayer and Devotion

In many traditions, sincere prayer is a method of opening the heart and invoking support from divine or cosmic forces.

ESOTERIC SYSTEMS AND PHILOSOPHIES

Esoteric philosophies can provide structure to comprehend the relationship between the soul and the cosmos. Often, they emphasise the inherent divinity of each being, and the universal oneness that underpins existence.

Theosophy

Initiated by Helena Blavatsky, Theosophy presents a cosmology in which every individual harbours an inner divine spark, intrinsically linked to the universe's sacred design.

Students of Theosophy explore concepts like karma, reincarnation, and spiritual evolution, gradually uncovering their cosmic soul and recognising its place within a grand, intelligent cosmos.

Hermeticism

Hermetic teachings, brought to popular attention by texts such as The Kybalion, suggest that the soul originates from a divine source and can reconnect with the cosmic mind through dedicated spiritual work.

Central to Hermetic philosophy is the idea "As above, so below," implying that the cosmic realm and the human microcosm reflect one another. By contemplating these principles, seekers can deepen their bond with the divine essence within themselves.

Anthroposophy (Rudolf Steiner's teachings) similarly emphasise humanity's spiritual evolution, offering additional perspectives on how the cosmic soul interacts with material existence.

Sound Healing & Music

Sound and vibration can serve as powerful tools for aligning with the soul. Certain frequencies believed to activate heightened states of awareness and foster deep spiritual communion.

Sound healing instruments can enhance our multidimensional well-being by creating a harmonious experience that gently and lovingly awakens all layers of our luminous energy field—body, mind, spirit and soul.

Instruments used in a sound healing bath, can include Crystal bowls, which are attuned to specific chakras, chimes, bells, gongs, and drums, which bathing you in sound resonance, helping to attune you to the united cosmos you are part of.

Sound Baths can facilitate deep healing. When crystal and Tibetan singing bowls are played together, dissonant tones can help release emotional pressure, while harmonious tones help to calm the mind and body.

Tuning forks, when used by a trained healer, can shift energy within the body and shamanic drumming, with a specific beat pattern can be especially powerful, enabling individuals to enter altered state of conscious awareness.

Solfeggio Frequencies

Ancient Solfeggio frequencies, notably 528Hz (sometimes called the "love frequency"), are said to resonate with both the cosmos and the human energy field. Practitioners report that listening to or chanting at these frequencies supports emotional healing, chakra balancing, and spiritual awakening, making it easier to access the cosmic aspect of the self.

Sacred Sound Practices

Traditions worldwide, from Gregorian chants to Tibetan singing bowls and Aboriginal didgeridoo ceremonies, have long utilised sound for spiritual elevation. The reverberations of these sacred instruments are thought to bypass the analytical mind, inducing meditative states where one can sense or directly perceive the presence of the cosmic soul.

Mantra Chanting

Incorporating mantra chanting, such as "Om" or "Aum", into daily practice, can bridge your consciousness and the universal vibration. This encourages a lived experience of cosmic unity.

Krystal Tones

When the tones of KA RA YA SA TA AA LA (KRYSTAL) are woven into a complete pattern, they can activate the LightBody. By sounding or communicating with these tones through meditation, prayer, music, or breathwork, individuals can refocus their minds and break through limiting beliefs and programs. These seven tones are specifically designed for heart and core healing, helping to reintegrate mental fragmentation. To listen to these tones visit our website at: themultidimensionalsoul.com/free-resources/

Astrology & Cosmology

Astrological insights and cosmological frameworks can illuminate the soul's interplay with universal forces. In turn, this can guide you to a fuller comprehension of your divine purpose.

Astrology and Soul Mapping

In systems such as Vedic astrology and evolutionary astrology, the positions of celestial bodies at key life events mirror the soul's evolutionary path.

These readings aim to reveal one's karmic lessons, strengths, and potential for spiritual growth, linking personal experiences with the broader cosmic dance. Understanding one's astrological chart can thus serve as a means to align more consciously with the cosmic soul.

Cosmology and Quantum Physics

Contemporary thinkers like Deepak Chopra and Carl Jung have explored how quantum physics and the collective unconscious might interweave with spiritual principles.

This interplay suggests that consciousness, including the cosmic soul, could exist as a fundamental force within the quantum field. From this perspective, the soul transcends time, space, and physical boundaries, offering a vision of reality where all things are interconnected in a vast cosmic web.

"Synchronicity", coined by Carl Jung, highlights meaningful coincidences that may point to underlying cosmic principles. This can reinforce the idea that your consciousness is intricately entangled with universal patterns.

Intuitive & Divination Tools

Divination and intuitive practices help a person access knowledge and insight from higher realms, peeling back layers of the psyche to expose the cosmic essence of the soul.

Tarot & Oracle Cards

Tarot readers often describe the cards as conduits for universal wisdom. Archetypal symbolism can guide seekers towards revelation about their life's purpose and spiritual trajectory.

In this sense, each reading can be seen as a dialogue with the cosmic soul. It offers clarity as to how the divine self can expresses itself, through life's challenges and opportunities.

Akashic Records

Often referred to as the energetic archive of every soul's journey, the Akashic Records provide a meditative or intuitive pathway into one's karmic lessons and destiny.

By accessing the Records under the guidance of a trained practitioner, individuals can potentially gain profound insights into their cosmic nature and the overarching plan of their soul's evolution.

Pendulum Dowsing

Utilised for yes/no queries, this simple technique can strengthen intuition and affirm one's ability to tap into subtle energies.

Runes and I Ching

These ancient oracles similarly offer windows into the soul's unfolding journey within the cosmic framework.

Energy Work & Healing Practices

Energy-based modalities promote alignment between the soul and universal energy, enabling a more direct experience of divine consciousness.

Reiki and Energy Healing

In Reiki, practitioners channel healing Universal Source energy through their crown chakra, which is then sent to the client through the practitioners palms placed on or above the client's body, clearing and balancing the chakra centers and releasing any energetic blockages that can hamper spiritual growth and connection with the cosmic soul. By addressing energetic imbalances, individuals may sense deeper levels of tranquillity and alignment; opening themselves to more profound communion with divine awareness.

Chakra Work

Focusing on the crown chakra (Sahasrara) and third-eye chakra (Ajna) can be especially beneficial in fostering cosmic awareness. Guided visualisations, sound healing, or crystal therapies targeting these energy centres can expand your perception of subtle realms, allowing the cosmic soul's presence to be felt more vividly.

Pranic Healing

Life-force energy via breathing exercises is used to harmonise your body, mind, and spirit.

Spiritual Communities & Teachings

Joining or learning from spiritual communities can enrich your exploration of the cosmic soul. A sense of community for a shared purpose of exploring the wisdom on the ancients, as well as providing each other support across organised practices.

Sufism

In Sufi mysticism, the practice of whirling, chanting, and ecstatic dance aims to dissolve the ego into the divine (fana). This direct experience of unity with the Beloved (God) mirrors the cosmic awareness that spiritual seekers strive to embody.

Through poetry (e.g., the works of Rumi) and devotion, Sufis open themselves to the flow of love and compassion, reflecting the essence of the cosmic soul.

New Age Spirituality

Encompassing a broad spectrum of beliefs, New Age teachings often highlight the interconnectedness of all beings, the ascension of consciousness, and the activation of light bodies. Practitioners may engage in guided meditations, channellings, and energy transmissions to awaken their cosmic potential and align more closely with divine wisdom.

Visualisation & Energy Alignment Techniques

Visualisation and energy alignment methods serve as cornerstones for those keen on deepening their connection with the cosmic soul, to transverse to higher realms of awareness.

Guided Visualisation

Guided imagery often involves journeys through celestial landscapes or encounters with beings of light. These internal adventures can bypass ordinary mental barriers, enabling participants to glimpse their higher self or cosmic essence.

In some cases, engaging with spirit guides or ascended masters in visualisations provides reassurance and guidance for ongoing spiritual development.

Sacred Geometry

Sacred geometry, including patterns like the Flower of Life, Metatron's Cube, or the Sri Yantra, symbolises the universe's underlying harmonic structure. By meditating upon these patterns, individuals can attune their consciousness to the order and harmony of creation, fostering a closer alignment with their cosmic soul.

Visualising these symbols during meditation can be an especially potent way to integrate cosmic awareness into daily life.

Crystal Grid Work

Arranging crystals in sacred geometric formations can amplify intentions and foster deeper energetic alignments.

Merkaba Activation   *Appendix III*

In some traditions, visualising the Merkaba, a light-body structure, supports ascension practices and contact with higher dimensional fields.

ABOUT
THE MULTIDIMENSIONAL SOUL

The Multidimensional Soul, created by Phillip and Leah, is an online portal designed to support individuals on their spiritual awakening journey. It aims to empower them in developing their intuitive gifts and accelerating their spiritual growth by offering a 5th-dimensional perspective.

Visit our website, **TheMultidimensionalSoul.com** where you will find live trainings and many of the meditations in this book. We are always adding to our library of videos!

Follow us on:
Facebook: @the.multidimensional.soul
Instagram: @the_multidimensional_soul
TikTok: @themultidimensionalsoul1
YouTube: @themultidimensionalsoul1292

ABOUT THE AUTHORS

Leah and Phillip are spiritual guides, healers, and visionaries dedicated to empowering individuals on their journey of spiritual awakening. With a shared mission to support planetary and human evolution, they created The Multidimensional Soul, an online portal offering tools, teachings, and guidance for intuitive development, personal transformation, and deep inner healing.

Leah brings a compassionate and intuitive approach, drawing on her gifts as an energy healer and her deep understanding of balancing the divine feminine and masculine energies. Her work focuses on helping others awaken their heart-light, embrace their authentic selves, and live with purpose and alignment.

Phillip is a spiritual teacher and mentor with profound access to multidimensional realms, allowing him to bring insights and wisdom from higher states of consciousness. His teachings inspire others to shift their perspectives, break free from limiting beliefs, and step into their highest potential. By connecting individuals with 5th-dimensional consciousness, he guides them to cultivate presence, embrace the NOW moment, and co-create a fulfilling future.

Together, Leah and Phillip combine their unique gifts to guide individual from simply surviving to truly living, helping them connect with their divine essence and contribute to the collective evolution of universal love.

To learn more visit: **themultidimensionalsoul.com**

NOTES